The Old Fashioned Rules of Spelling Book

The no-nonsense, proudly old-fashioned rules of spelling, which if they are followed, will help you to spell correctly

 Ward Lock Educational Co. Ltd.

WARD LOCK EDUCATIONAL CO. LTD.
LING KEE HOUSE
1 CHRISTOPHER ROAD
EAST GRINSTEAD
SUSSEX RH19 3BT
UNITED KINGDOM

A MEMBER OF THE LING KEE GROUP
HONG KONG · SINGAPORE · LONDON · NEW YORK

Text © Alan Jamieson

First published – 1980
Reprinted – 1981, 1983, 1992, 1995

ISBN 0-7062-4085-5

Other titles in this series:
The Old Fashioned Rules of Punctuation Book
ISBN 0 7062 4123 1
The Old Fashioned Rules of Grammar Book
ISBN 0 7062 3850 8
The Old Fashioned Handwriting Book
ISBN 0 7062 4139 8
The Old Fashioned Multiplication Book
ISBN 0 7062 4121 5
The Old Fashioned Division Book
ISBN 0 7062 4122 3
The Old Fashioned Adding-Up Book
ISBN 0 7062 4086 3
The Old Fashioned Taking-Away Book
ISBN 0 7062 4148 7
The Old Fashioned Mental Arithmetic Book
ISBN 0 7062 4160 6
The Old Fashioned Times Table Book
ISBN 0 7062 3749 8

Printed in Hong Kong

Contents

Words, words, words 4

Know your alphabet 5

Adding an *e* 6

Words ending in silent *e* : Rule 1 7

Words ending in silent *e* : Rule 2 8

Words with *ie* and *ei* 9

Doubling the final consonant : Rule 1 10

Doubling the final consonant : Rule 2 11

Words ending in *-ful* 12

Words ending in *y* (see also page 18) 13

Words with *qu* 14

Silent letters 15

Plurals 1 : Adding *s* 16

Plurals 2 : Words ending in s, x, o,
        ch, sh, z and zz 17

Plurals 3 : Words ending in *y* 18

Plurals 4 : Words ending in *f* or *fe* 19

Plurals 5 : Special plurals 20

Compound words 21

Prefixes 22

Suffixes 23

Confusing words and spellings 24

Words, words, words

There are almost half a million words in the English language. If you had to sit down and learn to spell ten words a day it would take you a lifetime to learn them all.

Instead, there are rules which can help you to spell correctly. By working through this book, you will learn some simple rules, and you will be able to spell many of the words you use every day. Rules and patterns account for over 80 per cent of all English words, so follow these rules carefully. And remember that because 'practice makes perfect' you should do plenty of writing, checking your spelling as you go.

Know your alphabet

If you cannot remember how to spell a word, *look it up* in a dictionary. Words in a dictionary are in alphabetical order starting with words beginning with *a*, then *b, c, d* and so on.

Write down the capital and small letters of the alphabet:

A . . . .   a . . . .   N . . . .   n . . . .

B . . . .   b . . . .   O . . . .   o . . . .

C . . . .   c . . . .   P . . . .   p . . . .

D . . . .   d . . . .   Q . . . .   q . . . .

E . . . .   e . . . .   R . . . .   r . . . .

F . . . .   f . . . .   S . . . .   s . . . .

G . . . .   g . . . .   T . . . .   t . . . .

H . . . .   h . . . .   U . . . .   u . . . .

I . . . .   i . . . .   V . . . .   v . . . .

J . . . .   j . . . .   W . . . .   w . . . .

K . . . .   k . . . .   X . . . .   x . . . .

L . . . .   l . . . .   Y . . . .   y . . . .

M . . . .   m . . . .   Z . . . .   z . . . .

Adding an e

When you add a silent *e* to the end of a word,
the sound and meaning of the word changes.
Look at these examples:

cap + e = cape   not + e = note

Add an *e* to these words and
say each word out loud.
The first one is done for you.

hat + e **hate** ....

pin + e ....

cod + e ....

cut + e ....

tap + e ....

rid + e ....

rod + e ....

cub + e ....

fat + e ....

fin + e ....

Can you make up any other
pairs of words like this?

Words ending in silent e

Rule 1

When a word ends in a silent *e,* you drop the *e* before adding an ending which begins with a vowel.

Here are some word endings which begin with a vowel:

-ed   -er   -ing   -en   -ous

Now try these:
The first one is done for you.

wipe   + ing   **wiping**..................

taste   + ed   ....

rule   + er   ....

fame   + ous   ....

take   + en   ....

write   + ing   ....

hope   + ed   ....

dance   + er   ....

joke   + ing   ....

Can you think of any exceptions to this rule?

Words ending in silent e

Rule 2

When a word ends in -*ce* or -*ge,* you keep the *e* when adding -*ous* or -*able*.

Here is an example:

change + able   changeable

Now try these:

service   + able   . . . .

courage   + ous   . . . .

peace   + able   . . . .

notice   + able   . . . .

manage   + able   . . . .

advantage + ous   . . . .

outrage   + ous   . . . .

**Make a list of ten more words
ending in -*ce* and -*ge,* and
then add either -*able* or -*ous* to them.**

Words with *ie* and *ei*

Remember when *ie* and *ei* sound like *ee* as in *keep,* then *i* comes before *e* except after *c*.

Here are some *ie* words:

field   yield   niece

Here are some *ei* words:

receive   ceiling   conceit

Spell these words
using *ie* or *ei*:

bel . . . . ve   rec . . . . pt   br . . . . f

p . . . . ce   ach . . . . ve   ch . . . . f

sh . . . . ld   dec . . . ve   th . . . . f

Remember the rule works when
ie or *ei* rhyme with *ee*. In
some words such as *eighteen* and
eiderdown, ei
sounds different again.

Spell these words correctly
using *ie* or *ei*:

. . . . ght   n . . . . ghbour   w . . . . ght

fr . . . . nd   h . . . . ght   for . . . . gn

There are exceptions to this such as *weird* and
seize. Can you think of any more?

Doubling the final consonant

Rule 1

In many words of one syllable ending in a single consonant preceded by a single vowel the consonant is doubled before adding *ed, er, est* or *ing*.

Look at these examples:

rob + er = robber

run + ing = running

Now try these:

stab + ed ....

tin + ed ....

swim + ing ....

fat + er ....

beg + ing ....

big + est ....

thin + est ....

hot + er ....

Remember that the final consonant is not doubled when it is preceded by two vowels or another consonant, such as:

feel + ing = feeling
halt + ing = halting
10

Doubling the final consonant

Rule 2

When a word ends in a vowel followed by the
letter *l,* you double the *l* before adding *ed, ing*
or *er.*

Look at this example:

level + ing = levelling

Now try these:

quarrel + ed ....

travel + ing ....

travel + er ....

label + ing ....

rebel + ed ....

tunnel + ing ....

signal + ed ....

cancel + ing ....

Parallel and *paralleled* are exceptions to the
rule. Can you think of any other exceptions?

Words ending in -ful

When *-full* is added to a word you change *-full* to *-ful*.

Look at this example:

help + full = helpful

Now try these:

use + full ....

wonder + full ....

cheer + full ....

care + full ....

thought + full ....

hope + full ....

peace + full ....

success + full ....

rest + full ....

Remember that if *-ly* is added to a word ending in *-ful* the word has two *l*s, as in *fully* and *carefully*.

Words ending in y
(see also page 18)

When a word ends in a consonant followed by a *y*, you change the *y* to *i* before a word ending such as *ed*.

Here are some word endings:

-ed -er -est -ment -ly -age

Now try these:
The first one is done for you.

dry   + ed   dried ....

dry   + er   ....

marry   + age   ....

supply + ed   ....

carry   + age   ....

tidy   + ly   ....

easy   + ly   ....

merry   + ment ....

try   + ed   ....

angry   + ly   ....

Remember to keep the *y* if it is preceded by a vowel.
Do you know any exceptions to the rule?

13

Words with qu

Remember that the letter *q* in a word is always followed by *u* and a vowel.

Here are some *qu* words:

quick   quiet   request   enquire   unique

Make a list of words with the letters *qu* at the beginning or in the middle.

. . . .

. . . .

. . . .

. . . .

. . . .

. . . .

. . . .

. . . .

. . . .

. . . .

. . . .

Check your spellings in a dictionary.

Words with silent letters

Many words contain a silent letter which can be at the beginning, middle or end of a word.

The letters which are sometimes silent are:

g **as in sign**

k **as in knife**

w **as in wrist**

h **as in hour**

c **as in scissors**

p **as in psalm**

n **as in hymn**

b **as in lamb**

u **as in biscuit**

t **as in listen**

Make a list of words which have a silent letter in them.

. . . .

. . . .

. . . .

. . . .

. . . .

Check your spellings in a dictionary.

Plurals 1

Adding *s* to make the plural

For most singular nouns the plural is formed by adding *s*.

Here is an example:

railway + s = railways

By adding *s*, write the plural of a word for each letter of the alphabet.
The first one is done for you.

a **acorns**

b ....

c ....

d ....

e ....

f ....

g ....

h ....

i ....

j ....

k ....

l ....

m ....

n ....

o ....

p ....

q ....

r ....

s ....

t ....

u ....

v ....

w ....

x ....

y ....

z ....

Check your spellings in a dictionary.

16

Plurals 2

Words ending in *s, x, o, ch, sh, z* and *zz*

When a word ends in *o, s, x, ch, zz, sh* or *z* you add *es* to make the plural.

Here are some examples:

fox — foxes   pass — passes

Write out the plural of these words:

box   . . . .

witch   . . . .

kiss   . . . .

thrush   . . . .

buzz   . . . .

dish   . . . .

watch   . . . .

hero   . . . .

peach   . . . .

cargo   . . . .

six   . . . .

For some words ending in *-o* you add *s* to make the plural, as in *photos, pianos*. Can you think of any more words ending in *os?*

Plurals 3

Words ending in *y*

When a word ends in *y* and is preceded by a consonant, to make the plural you change the *y* to *ie* before adding *s*.

Look at this example:

lady + s = ladies

Now try these:

baby + s ....

party + s ....

fly + s ....

lorry + s ....

duty + s ....

country + s ....

diary + s ....

library + s ....

fairy + s ....

puppy + s ....

Remember for words ending in a vowel and a *y* you keep the *y* before adding *s* to make the plural, as in valley + s = valleys

toy + s = toys

Plurals 4

Words ending in *f* or *fe*

To make the plural of most words which end in *f* or *fe*, you change the *f* or *fe* to *v* and add *es*.

Look at this example:

wolf — wolves

Write out the plurals of these words:

loaf ....

calf ....

wife ....

shelf ....

elf ....

thief ....

scarf ....

knife ....

life ....

leaf ....

The exceptions to this rule simply add *s*
to make the plural, as in:

roof   — roofs

chief   — chiefs

giraffe — giraffes

Can you think of any more?

Plurals 5

Special plurals

Remember that some words such as *sheep* do not change to make the plural. The plurals of other words need to be memorized very carefully.

Write the plurals of these words:

child . . . .

aircraft . . . .

tooth . . . .

salmon . . . .

mouse . . . .

goose . . . .

foot . . . .

deer . . . .

ox . . . .

plateau . . . .

grouse . . . .

oasis . . . .

Check your answers in a dictionary.

Compound words

A compound word is made by joining two words together to make a new word.

Here is an example:

any + thing = anything

Choose different pairs of words from these to make compound words:

some	held	with	up
hill	ward	class	body
thing	room	any	to

. . . .

. . . .

. . . .

. . . .

. . . .

. . . .

. . . .

. . . .

Prefixes

A group of letters added to the beginning of a word to make a new word is called a *prefix*.

Look at this example:

un + happy = unhappy

Here are some more prefixes:

mis-   dis-   re-   fore-
for-   anti-   sub-   ante-

Write three words beginning with each of these prefixes:

mis-   . . . .

dis-   . . . .

re-   . . . .

fore-   . . . .

ante-   . . . .

sub-   . . . .

anti-   . . . .

for-   . . . .

un-   . . . .

Check the spellings and meanings in a dictionary.

Suffixes

A group of letters added on to the end of a main word is called a *suffix*.

Look at this example:

loud + ly = loudly

Here are some more suffixes:

-ed   -ful   -less   -ing
-ance -ence -ness -able

Write three words which end
with each of these suffixes:

.... **-ed**

.... **-ful**

.... **-less**

.... **-ing**

.... **-ance**

.... **-ence**

.... **-ness**

.... **-able**

Check your spellings in a dictionary.

Confusing words and spellings

Many words sound alike but are spelt differently. Learn these words separately and check their meaning in a dictionary.

Look at this example:

bare — to be without clothes
bear — a wild animal

Write a sentence using each of these words to show the correct meaning:

buy   ....

by   ....

dear   ....

deer   ....

peace   ....

piece   ....

scent   ....

sent   ....

pair   ....

pear   ....

pain   ....

pane   ....

Check your answers in a dictionary.